DK SUPER History

SUSAN B ANTHONY AND WOMEN'S RIGHTS

Find out all about Susan B Anthony and her pivotal role in the American women's suffrage movement

PRODUCED FOR DK BY
Editorial Just Content Limited
Design Studio Noel

Author Jennifer Kaul

Senior Editor Ankita Awasthi Tröger
Editor Hattie Hansford
Senior Art Editor Gilda Pacitti
Graphic Story Illustrator Matt Garbutt
Managing Editor Carine Tracanelli
Managing Art Editor Sarah Corcoran
Pre-Production Coordinator Shanker Prasad
Pre-Production Designer Jaypal Chauhan
Production Controller Rebecca Parton
Publisher Sarah Forbes
Managing Director, Learning Hilary Fine

First published in Great Britain in 2025 by
Dorling Kindersley Limited
20 Vauxhall Bridge Road,
London SW1V 2SA

The authorised representative in the EEA is
Dorling Kindersley Verlag GmbH. Arnulfstr. 124,
80636 Munich, Germany

10 9 8 7 6 5 4 3 2 1
001–350121–Sep/2025

A CIP catalogue record for this book
is available from the British Library.
ISBN: 978-0-2417-4478-9

Printed and bound in China

www.dk.com

This book was made with Forest Stewardship Council™ certified paper – one small step in DK's commitment to a sustainable future.
Learn more at www.dk.com/uk/information/sustainability

Contents

Words in **bold** are explained in the glossary on page 44.

History in Perspective

Susan B Anthony played a very important role in the fight to secure voting rights for women.

Today, all American **citizens** over the age of 18 have the right to **vote**. However, this was not always the case. Certain groups were left out of decision-making in the United States. Historically, people were prevented from voting for reasons including race, religion and gender. This started to change for American women in 1920. Almost 150 years after the nation was founded, many women finally gained the right to vote.

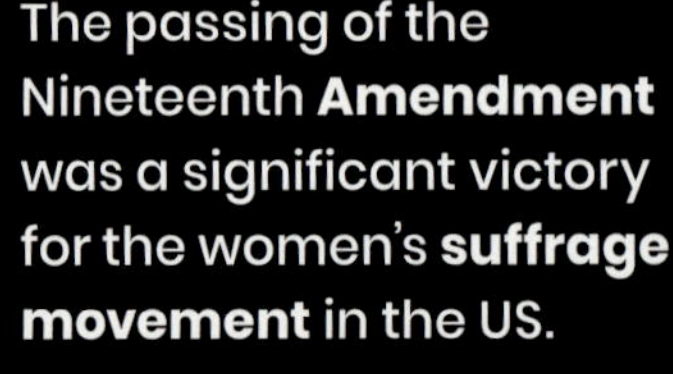

The passing of the Nineteenth **Amendment** was a significant victory for the women's **suffrage movement** in the US.

Where and when?

The Nineteenth Amendment gave American women the right to vote. It was passed on 4 June 1919, by the **House of Representatives** in Washington, DC. On 18 August 1920, the amendment became law.

Many people, especially women, worked tirelessly for the rights that all American adults now enjoy.

Think about it

We use documents and other **sources** to learn about history. How might these help us learn about the women's rights movement?

Who was involved?

Susan B Anthony spent most of her life **campaigning** for women's suffrage. It was not easy. The views of people in the past were very different from the views of people today. Many people were **opposed** to the idea that women should have the right to vote. It took decades of work from **suffragists** and other campaigners to secure women's suffrage.

Different perspectives

Different groups in society may have deeply contrasting experiences of events. Official records of the past often only present one side of the story. This means that they can't reflect the experiences of everyone affected. To understand what happened, it is important that we look at events from more than one point of view.

Key Events
WHAT HAPPENED WHEN

The women's rights movement involved many important milestones. Many of them relate to the life of Susan B Anthony.

1820

10 MAY

Anthony is born in Adams, Massachusetts. She is one of seven siblings. Her family is very religious and have a strong sense of justice.

1848

19–20 JULY

The first women's rights **convention** is organised by Elizabeth Cady Stanton and Lucretia Mott. It is held in Seneca Falls, New York.

Our Roll of Honor
Containing all the
Signatures to the "Declaration of Sentiments"
Set Forth by the First
Woman's Rights Convention,
held at
Seneca Falls, New York
July 19-20, 1848

LADIES:

Lucretia Mott	Sophronia Taylor	Rachel D. Bonnel
Harriet Cady Eaton	Cynthia Davis	Betsey Tewksbury
Margaret Pryor	Hannah Plant	Rhoda Palmer
Elizabeth Cady Stanton	Lucy Jones	Margaret Jenkins
Eunice Newton Foote	Sarah Whitney	Cynthia Fuller
Mary Ann M'Clintock	Mary H. Hallowell	Mary Martin
Margaret Schooley	Elizabeth Conklin	P. A. Culvert
Martha C. Wright	Sally Pitcher	Susan R. Doty
Jane C. Hunt	Mary Conklin	Rebecca Race
Amy Post	Susan Quinn	Sarah A. Mosher
Catherine F. Stebbins	Mary S. Mirror	Mary E. Vail
Mary Ann Frink	Phebe King	Lucy Spalding
Lydia Mount	Julia Ann Drake	Lovina Latham
Delia Mathews	Charlotte Woodward	Sarah Smith
Catherine C. Paine	Martha Underhill	Eliza Martin
Elizabeth W. M'Clintock	Dorothy Mathews	Maria E. Wilbur
Malvina Seymour	Eunice Barker	Elizabeth D. Smith
Phebe Mosher	Sarah R. Woods	Caroline Barker
Catherine Shaw	Lydia Gild	Ann Porter
Deborah Scott	Sarah Hoffman	Experience Gibbs
Sarah Hallowell	Elizabeth Leslie	Antoinette E. Segur
Mary M'Clintock	Martha Ridley	Hannah J. Latham
Mary Gilbert		Sarah Sisson

GENTLEMEN:

Richard P. Hunt	William S. Dell	Nathan J. Milliken
Samuel D. Tillman	James Mott	S. E. Woodworth
Justin Williams	William Burroughs	Edward F. Underhill
Elisha Foote	Robert Smallbridge	George W. Pryor
Frederick Douglass	Jacob Mathews	Joel Bunker
Henry W. Seymour	Charles L. Hoskins	Isaac VanTassel
Henry Seymour	Thomas M'Clintock	Thomas Dell
David Spalding	Saron Phillips	E. W. Capron
William G. Barker	Jacob P. Chamberlain	Stephen Shear
Elias J. Doty	Jonathan Metcalf	Henry Hatley
John Jones		Azaliah Schooley

1851

12 MAY

Anthony meets Stanton. They become lifelong friends who work towards women's suffrage and other rights.

1866

10 MAY

Anthony and Stanton found the American Equal Rights **Association**. They start its publication, *The Revolution*.

1869

26 FEBRUARY

The Fifteenth Amendment is passed by **Congress**. Anthony and Stanton oppose this because it does not guarantee suffrage for women.

15 MAY

Anthony and Stanton form the National Woman Suffrage Association.

1872

5 NOVEMBER

Anthony illegally votes in the presidential **election**. She is arrested two weeks later.

1890

18 FEBRUARY

Anthony, Stanton and other supporters of women's suffrage start the National American Woman Suffrage Association.

1906

13 MARCH

Anthony dies of heart failure and pneumonia in Rochester, New York. She is 86 years old.

1920

26 AUGUST

The Nineteenth Amendment is formally added to the US **Constitution**. It gives some women the right to vote. However, women from marginalised communities still face a fight to be included in the vote.

Key People
WHO'S WHO

The fight for women's right to vote involved many people. They campaigned tirelessly across the United States over many decades.

Supporters

Frederick Douglass

Frederick Douglass
A Black **abolitionist** and supporter of women's suffrage. He was formerly **enslaved**. Later, he wrote three autobiographies of his life.

William Lloyd Garrison
An abolitionist. He founded an anti-slavery newspaper called *The Liberator.* Once **slavery** was **abolished** in the United States, he became a vocal supporter of women's rights.

Opponents and politicians

Josephine Dodge
An **anti-suffragist**. She founded the National Association Opposed to Woman Suffrage. She felt women could do more important work outside **politics**.

President Woodrow Wilson
The 28th president of the United States. He originally opposed the idea of women's suffrage, but ultimately supported it.

President Woodrow Wilson

Campaigners

Susan B Anthony
A leader of the women's suffrage movement. She helped found several women's rights organisations. Although she died 14 years before it took place, she is largely credited with the passing of the Nineteenth Amendment.

Elizabeth Cady Stanton
A leader of the women's rights movement. She helped organise the Seneca Falls Convention. She also helped form several women's rights organisations.

Alice Paul
A suffragist. She founded the National Woman's Party in 1916. She led the party for almost 60 years.

Lucretia Mott
An abolitionist and suffragist. She helped organise the Seneca Falls Convention. She became passionate about women's rights after attending an anti-slavery convention where only men were allowed to participate.

Lucy Stone
An abolitionist and suffragist. She helped found the American Woman Suffrage Association. Her speeches have been credited as inspiring Anthony to join the women's rights movement.

Sojourner Truth
A Black abolitionist and suffragist. She delivered a very famous speech about the movement called "Ain't I a Woman?"

Lucretia Mott

Elizabeth Cady Stanton

Key Location
SENECA FALLS

Over 19 and 20 July 1848, the first women's rights convention was held in Seneca Falls, New York. It was organised by Elizabeth Cady Stanton and Lucretia Mott. Its aim was to allow women the opportunity to discuss their rights, and for men to support them in achieving **equality**. The convention is seen as a **pivotal** event in establishing the women's rights and suffrage movements in the United States.

ONTARIO, NY

WHY SENECA FALLS?

Seneca Falls was chosen partly because Stanton lived there. Upstate New York had also been at the centre of the campaign for the **abolition** of slavery since the 1820s, and therefore many people who lived in the area had an interest in equal rights.

WESLEYAN CHAPEL

The Seneca Falls Convention took place in the Wesleyan Chapel. This church was a meeting place for **progressive** thinkers and **activists**, and had been used as a venue for anti-slavery discussions and political rallies. Other venues may not have been willing to host a women's rights convention, but the convention aligned with the progressive ideals of the leaders of the Wesleyan Methodist congregation.

SENECA FALLS CONVENTION

This cartoon depicts the convention taking place inside the Wesleyan Chapel. The event was advertised in a local newspaper and about 300 people attended. During this convention, Stanton introduced her Declaration of Sentiments. This was a document that listed the rights to which she believed women were entitled. One of the rights listed was women's suffrage.

SENECA FALLS
TERLOO
Waterloo
Seneca Falls
FAYETTE
Seneca, NY
VARICK
ROMULUS
OVID

A CHANCE MEETING

As commemorated by this statue in Seneca Falls, the town was also the location for the first introduction of Stanton to Susan B Anthony. In 1851, Anthony had come to Seneca Falls to hear the abolitionist William Lloyd Garrison speak. She was introduced to Stanton by Amelia Jenks Bloomer when they bumped into one another on a street corner. This started their friendship and important collaboration in the women's rights movement.

A Quaker Upbringing

Susan Brownell Anthony was born on 15 February 1820, in the town of Adams, Massachusetts. Her parents were Daniel and Lucy Anthony. Anthony's parents were supportive of her education. She learned to read and write when she was just three years old. When her family moved to New York in 1826, she started going to school.

Quakers had long believed in equality between men and women. They believed both boys and girls should receive an education. Women had always been allowed to speak in meetings, and many Quaker preachers were women.

FAMILY VALUES

Anthony's family were Quakers. Growing up, Anthony was exposed to many political discussions. Her parents were supporters of **temperance**. This movement aimed to **prohibit** the production and sale of alcohol in the United States. Anthony's parents also supported the abolition of slavery. On most Sundays, they used their home as a political meeting place. As a result, Anthony met important abolitionists like Frederick Douglass and William Lloyd Garrison.

This woodcut print depicts a 19th-century Quaker meeting.

Anthony worked as a headmistress and teacher before becoming an activist.

EARLY ACTIVISM

In 1848, while she was working as a teacher, Anthony became involved in the teacher's union. There, she learned that male teachers were paid $10 each month. Female teachers were paid $2.50. This went against the values of equality that Anthony had been taught growing up. The causes that her family championed would soon become important to her too.

Fascinating fact

Social reformers often came from religious groups such as the Quakers. In fact, the Quakers were the first religious movement to speak against slavery as early as 1688.

The Quaker movement, also known as the Religious Society of Friends, was founded in England in the 17th century by George Fox. Quakers played a key role in both the abolitionist and women's rights movements.

An Unjust Society

Many **injustices** affected American society in the early 1800s. Women had few rights compared to men, and only white men were allowed to vote in elections. However, arguably the gravest injustice was slavery. Up until 1865, it was still legal in some parts of the United States.

The abolitionist movement continued to grow throughout the 18th and 19th centuries. This photo shows members of the American Anti-Slavery Society. It was founded in 1833. Lucretia Mott is in the front row.

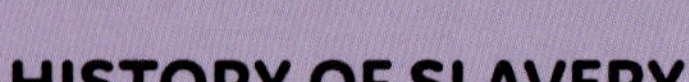

HISTORY OF SLAVERY

In the 1600s, enslaved labour had been used to help develop the British colonies. It continued in the United States for over 200 years more. Many people recognised the horrors of slavery. In the early 1800s, it was abolished in the North. However, states in the South depended on enslaved labour. They did not want slavery to be abolished.

TREATMENT OF WOMEN

Women had experienced unequal treatment throughout US history. In the early 1800s, most women were expected to marry, have children and manage their households. Married women were under the control of their husbands. They could not own property or manage the money they earned. Women were not allowed to vote. This meant they had no say in laws that limited their rights.

Single women and widows had more rights than married women at the time. Widows were respected members of society. Single women, however, were viewed with suspicion and given low-paying, **menial** jobs.

A NEW WORKFORCE

The American Industrial Revolution changed many women's lives. For the first time, a large number of women began to work outside of the home. Working in big groups together created a sense of female community. Working conditions were poor, and many women joined the labour movement to fight for better conditions.

The American Industrial Revolution took place in the late 18th and 19th centuries. **Industrialisation** increased the manufacture of goods and boosted the economy.

Fascinating fact

Abigail Adams was the wife of John Adams, who would become US president in 1797. She supported women's rights. In 1776, she wrote a letter to her husband to warn him that if "particular care and attention is not paid to the ladies" they would form a rebellion and ignore "laws in which we have no voice or representation".

The Fight for Change

By the 1840s, social movements in the United States were getting stronger. Abolitionists were helping enslaved people escape to freedom using the Underground Railroad. Women's rights activists were meeting in larger numbers and finding their voices.

The Underground Railroad worked in secret. If they were caught, enslaved people and anyone who helped them faced severe punishments.

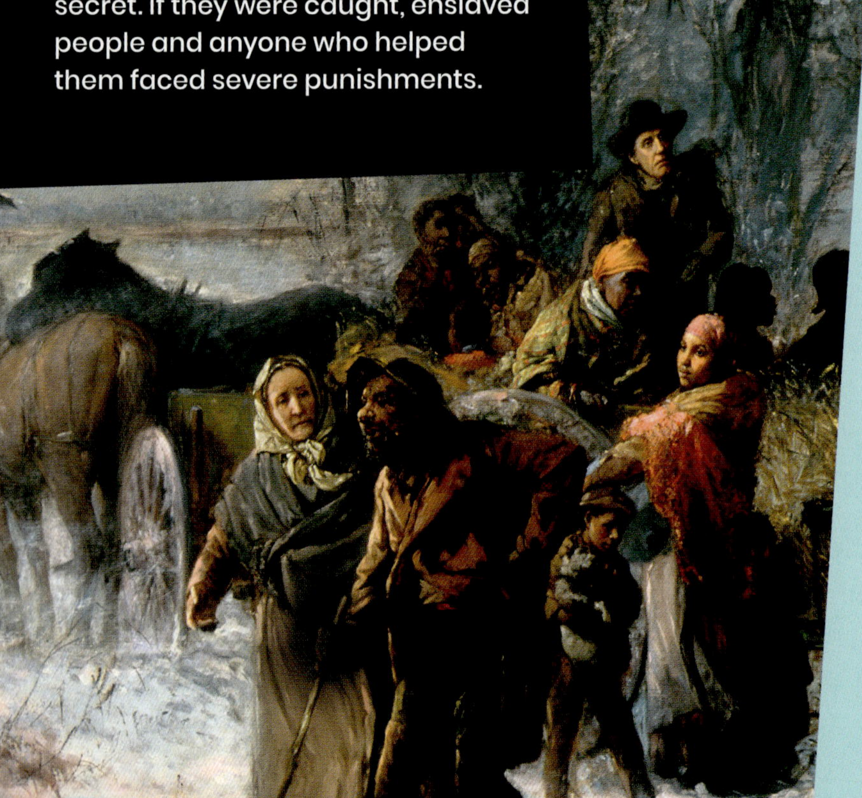

FIGHTING FOR FREEDOM

The Underground Railroad refers to the network of people who helped enslaved people travel north to freedom. They created routes and provided supplies to help enslaved people escape. The Underground Railroad included white and free Black American people. At the same time, people were gathering to discuss and campaign against slavery in the United States. Abolitionists held meetings, spoke publicly and wrote texts. Like Susan B Anthony, many abolitionists were Quakers.

The first World Anti-Slavery Convention was held in London in 1840.

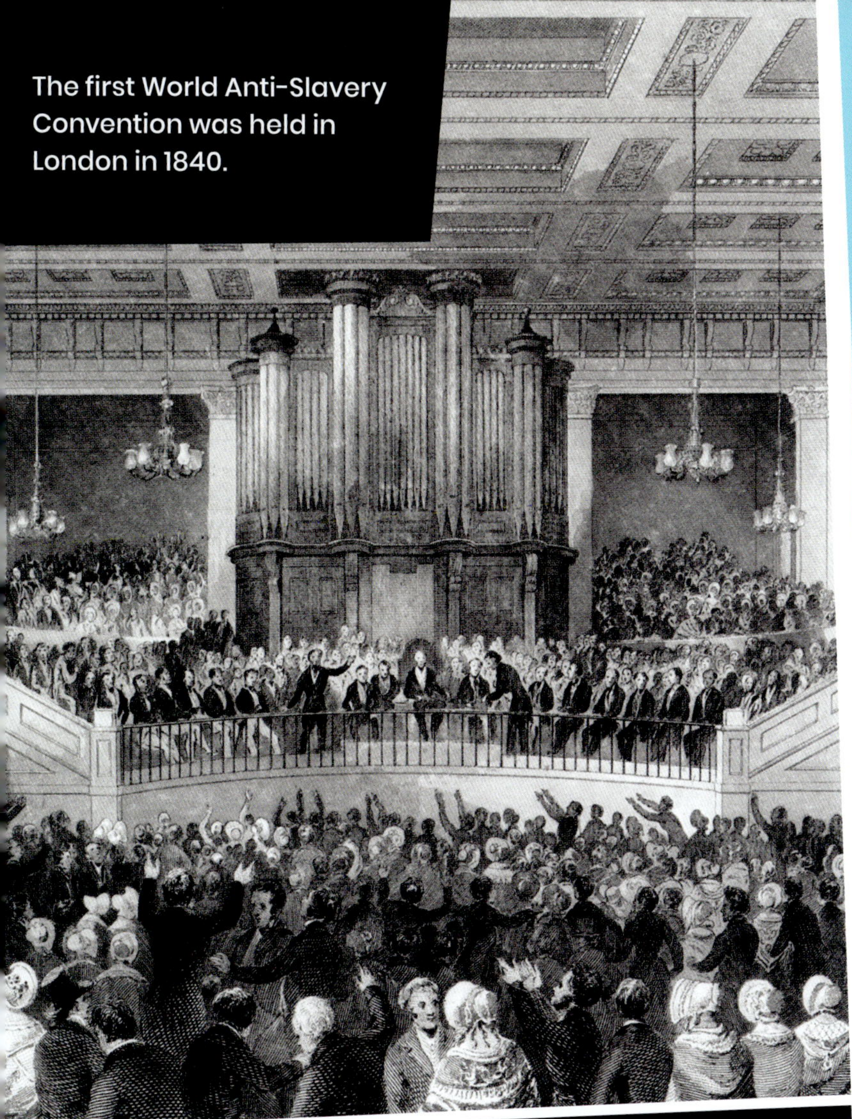

This engraving shows Stanton presenting her Declaration of Sentiments at the Seneca Falls Convention. One hundred people signed it to show their support.

THE WORLD ANTI-SLAVERY CONVENTION

Many female abolitionists worked towards rights for Black American people. At the same time, they faced **discrimination** because of their sex. In 1840, the first World Anti-Slavery Convention took place in London, England. This was a meeting of prominent abolitionists and many American activists attended. Lucretia Mott led the female **delegation** at the convention. However, women were not allowed to speak or vote, which meant she could not participate.

THE SENECA FALLS CONVENTION

Elizabeth Cady Stanton was also at the World Anti-Slavery Convention. She was frustrated by how Mott was treated. So, Mott and Stanton decided to organise a convention for women's rights. This was the Seneca Falls Convention, held in July 1848.

Think about it

Stanton based the Declaration of Sentiments on the **Declaration of Independence**. Why do you think she did this? How are the two documents similar?

A Lifelong Partnership

Susan B Anthony did not attend the Seneca Falls Convention, but she met Elizabeth Cady Stanton soon after. The two became lifelong friends and worked together in the women's rights movement for the rest of their lives.

A NEW CAUSE

When they met, Stanton was already a supporter of women's rights, whereas Anthony was more involved in the abolitionist and temperance movements. While attending a temperance convention in 1852, Anthony was refused the chance to speak because she was a woman. Instead, she was told to listen and learn. So, Anthony decided to start her own organisation. It was called the Woman's New York State Temperance Society. Stanton became its president. Soon after, Anthony and Stanton formed the New York State Woman's Rights Committee.

Stanton wrote about meeting Anthony for the first time in her journal. She described Anthony's **earnest** face and neat clothes and wrote that she liked her immediately.

AN INSPIRING SPEECH

In 1852, Anthony attended the third National Woman's Rights Convention in Syracuse, New York. Lucy Stone gave a powerful speech about women's rights at the convention. Stone's speech inspired Anthony to join the movement.

A POWERFUL DUO

Anthony and Stanton made a good team. Each brought her own set of talents to the movement. Stanton was a skilled writer, while Anthony was a strong speaker. Stanton had seven children, which made it hard for her to travel very often. Anthony, meanwhile, was single with no children. She could travel around the country, sharing the movement's ideas with different audiences.

Lucy Stone

Anthony travelled often and delivered as many as 75 to 100 speeches a year to **advocate** for women's rights.

Think about it ?

When describing her partnership with Anthony, Stanton once said, "I **forged** the thunderbolts, she fired them" (Griffith, 1984). What do you think she might have meant by this?

Pushing for Equal Rights

Susan B Anthony is best known for her work as a suffragist, but she worked towards other rights for women too. She started a **petition** in support of property rights for married women. She spoke in favour of education for women and all Black American people. She also continued her work as an abolitionist. As a result, she faced angry mobs and threats.

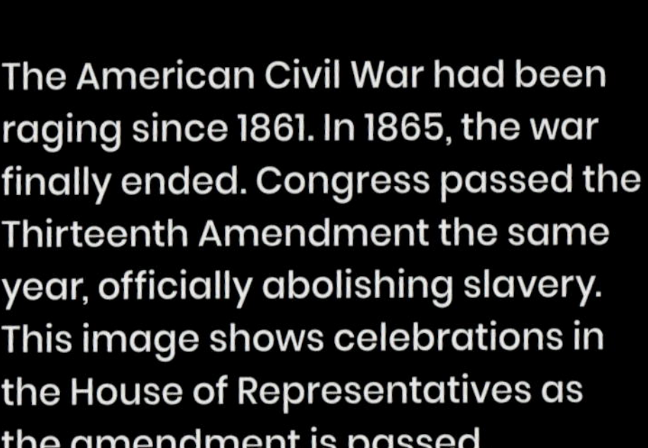

The American Civil War had been raging since 1861. In 1865, the war finally ended. Congress passed the Thirteenth Amendment the same year, officially abolishing slavery. This image shows celebrations in the House of Representatives as the amendment is passed.

AFTER ABOLITION

Now that abolition had been achieved, Anthony focused her attention on women's rights. In 1866, she and Elizabeth Cady Stanton founded the American Equal Rights Association. The goal of the association was to obtain equal rights for all American citizens. They created a weekly newspaper for the organisation. It was called *The Revolution*. The newspaper contained thoughts about marriage, divorce, equal pay, suffrage and more.

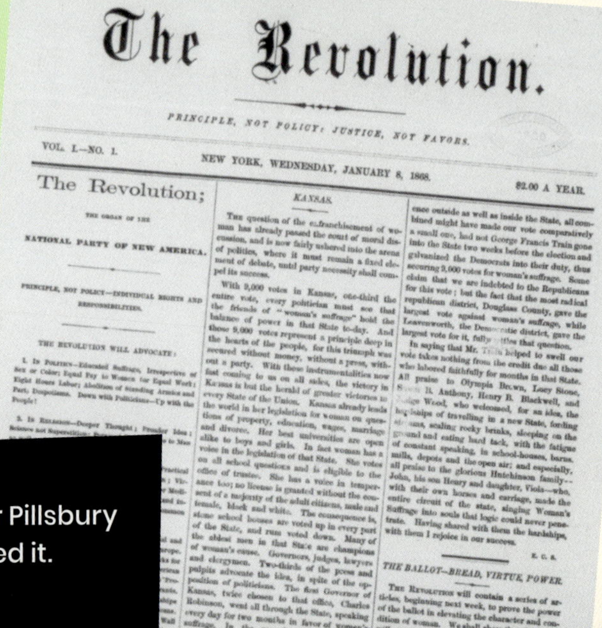

The Revolution.

PRINCIPLE, NOT POLICY: JUSTICE, NOT FAVORS.

VOL. I.—NO. 1. NEW YORK, WEDNESDAY, JANUARY 8, 1868. $2.00 A YEAR.

The Revolution;

THE ORGAN OF THE

NATIONAL PARTY OF NEW AMERICA.

PRINCIPLE, NOT POLICY—INDIVIDUAL RIGHTS AND RESPONSIBILITIES.

THE REVOLUTION WILL ADVOCATE:

1. In Politics—Educated Suffrage, Irrespective of Sex or Color; Equal Pay to Women for Equal Work; Eight Hours Labor; Abolition of Standing Armies and Party Despotisms. Down with Politicians—Up with the People!

2. In Religion—Deeper Thought; Proader Idea; Science not Superstition;

KANSAS.

The question of the enfranchisement of woman has already passed the court of moral discussion, and is now fairly ushered into the arena of politics, where it must remain a fixed element of debate, until party necessity shall compel its success.

With 9,000 votes in Kansas, one-third the entire vote, every politician must see that the friends of "woman's suffrage" hold the balance of power in that State to-day. And those 9,000 votes represent a principle deep in the hearts of the people, for this triumph was secured without money, without a press, without a party. With these instrumentalities now fast coming to us on all sides, the victory in Kansas is but the herald of greater victories in every State of the Union. Kansas already leads the world in her legislation for woman on questions of property, education, wages, marriage and divorce. Her best universities are open alike to boys and girls. In fact woman has a voice in the legislation of that State. She votes on all school questions and is eligible to the office of trustee. She has a voice in temperance too; no license is granted without the consent of a majority of the adult citizens, male and female, black and white. The consequence is, stone school houses are voted up in every part of the State, and rum voted down. Many of the ablest men in that State are champions of woman's cause. Governors, judges, lawyers and clergymen. Two-thirds of the press and pulpits advocate the idea, in spite of the opposition of politicians. The first Governor of Kansas, twice chosen to that office, Charles Robinson, went all through the State, speaking every day for two months in favor of woman's suffrage.

ence outside as well as inside the State, all combined might have made our vote comparatively a small one, had not George Francis Train gone into the State two weeks before the election and galvanized the Democrats into their duty, thus securing 9,000 votes for woman's suffrage. Some claim that we are indebted to the Republicans for this vote; but the fact that the most radical republican district, Douglass County, gave the largest vote against woman's suffrage, while Leavenworth, the Democratic district, gave the largest vote for it, fully settles that question.

In saying that Mr. Train helped to swell our vote takes nothing from the credit due all those who labored faithfully for months in that State. All praise to Olympia Brown, Lucy Stone, Susan B. Anthony, Henry B. Blackwell, and Judge Wood, who welcomed, for an idea, the hardships of travelling in a new State, fording streams, scaling rocky banks, sleeping on the ground and eating hard tack, with the fatigue of constant speaking, in school-houses, barns, mills, depots and the open air; and especially, all praise to the glorious Hutchinson family—John, his son Henry and daughter, Viola—who, with their own horses and carriage, made the entire circuit of the state, singing Woman's Suffrage into souls that logic could never penetrate. Having shared with them the hardships, with them I rejoice in our success.

E. C. S.

THE BALLOT—BREAD, VIRTUE, POWER.

The Revolution will contain a series of articles, beginning next week, to prove the power of the ballot in elevating the character and condition of woman.

Stanton and another activist named Parker Pillsbury edited the *The Revolution*. Anthony published it.

Sojourner Truth was another passionate advocate for abolition, temperance and women's rights. Truth was born enslaved but escaped. This painting shows Truth with President Abraham Lincoln in Washington, DC. She met him in 1864.

A FOCUS ON SUFFRAGE

Soon, Anthony and Stanton's primary focus was suffrage. They hoped to secure the right to vote for all people, regardless of their race, skin colour or sex. Anthony believed there would be no laws and **representatives** to serve women's interests until women had a say in American politics and government.

Think about it

Why did campaigners see the right to vote as the most important of the changes they were working towards?

THE NATIONAL WOMAN SUFFRAGE ASSOCIATION

In January 1869, Anthony and Stanton started the National Woman Suffrage Association. They began working towards the right to vote for women. Anthony gave many speeches. She also organised the first Woman Suffrage Convention in Washington, DC.

CONSTITUTION
OF THE
National Woman Suffrage Association.

ARTICLE 1.—This organization shall be called the National Woman Suffrage Association.

ARTICLE 2.—The object of this Association shall be to secure NATIONAL protection for women citizens in the exercise of their right to vote.

ARTICLE 3.—All citizens of the United States subscribing to this Constitution, and contributing not less than one dollar annually, shall be considered members of the Association, with the right to participate in its deliberations.

ARTICLE 4.—The officers of this Association shall be a President, a Vice-President from each of the States and Territories. Corresponding and Recording Secretaries, a Treasurer, an Executive Committee of not less than five, and an Advisory Committee consisting of one person from each State and Territory.

ARTICLE 5.—All Woman Suffrage Societies throughout the country shall be welcomed as auxiliaries; and their accredited officers or duly appointed representatives shall be recognized as members of the National Association.

OFFICERS OF THE NATIONAL WOMAN SUFFRAGE ASSOCIATION:

PRESIDENT.
ELIZABETH CADY STANTON, Tenafly, New Jersey.

VICE-PRESIDENTS.

Lucretia Mott, Ernestine L. Rose, Paulina Wright Davis, Clarinda I. H. Nichols, Amelia A. Bloomer, Mathilde Francesca Anneke, Virginia L. Minor, Catharine A. F. Stebbins, Julia & Abby Smith, Abby P. Ela,
Pa., N. Y., R. I., Cal., Iowa., Wis., Mo., Mich., Ct., N. H., Mass., Me.

Eliza D. Stewart, Mary H. Williams, Elizabeth Boynton Harbert, Sarah Burger Stearns, Ada W. Lucas, Helen E. Starrett, Ann L. Quinby, Eliz Avery Meriwether, Mrs. L. C. Locke, Emily P. Collins, Mary J. Spaulding, Mrs. P Holmes Drake,
Ohio., Ind., Ill., Minn., Neb., Kan., Ken., Ten., Texas., La., Geo., Ala.

Flora M. Wright, Frances Anne Pillsbury, Cynthia Anthony, Carrie F. Putnam, Anna Ella Carroll, A. J. Duniway, Hannah H. Clapp, Dr. Alida C. Avery, Mary O. Brown, Esther A. Morris, Annie Godbe,
Fla., S. C., N. C., Va., Md., Oregon., Nevada., Col., Wash. Ter., Wyoming Ter., Utah.

This constitution of the National Woman Suffrage Association was written in 1876. It lists the goals of the organisation and its members.

The Movement Splits

On 3 February 1870, the Fifteenth Amendment to the US Constitution was **ratified**. It gave all male citizens aged 21 years and older the right to vote, regardless of their race or previous enslavement. However, it did not extend the same right to women. This caused a split in the movement between those who supported this amendment and those who wanted universal suffrage.

This illustration was published in *Harper's Weekly* in 1867. It shows Black American men casting their vote for the first time.

CONFLICTING VIEWS

Susan B Anthony had been a strong advocate for equal rights for Black American people, but she did not support the Fifteenth Amendment. She and some other activists rejected it and campaigned against it. They saw it as an injustice to women and wanted universal suffrage instead.

This statue in Rochester, New York, is called *Let's Have Tea*. It shows Anthony talking with Frederick Douglass. They disagreed about the Fifteenth Amendment, as Douglass believed in getting rights for Black men first.

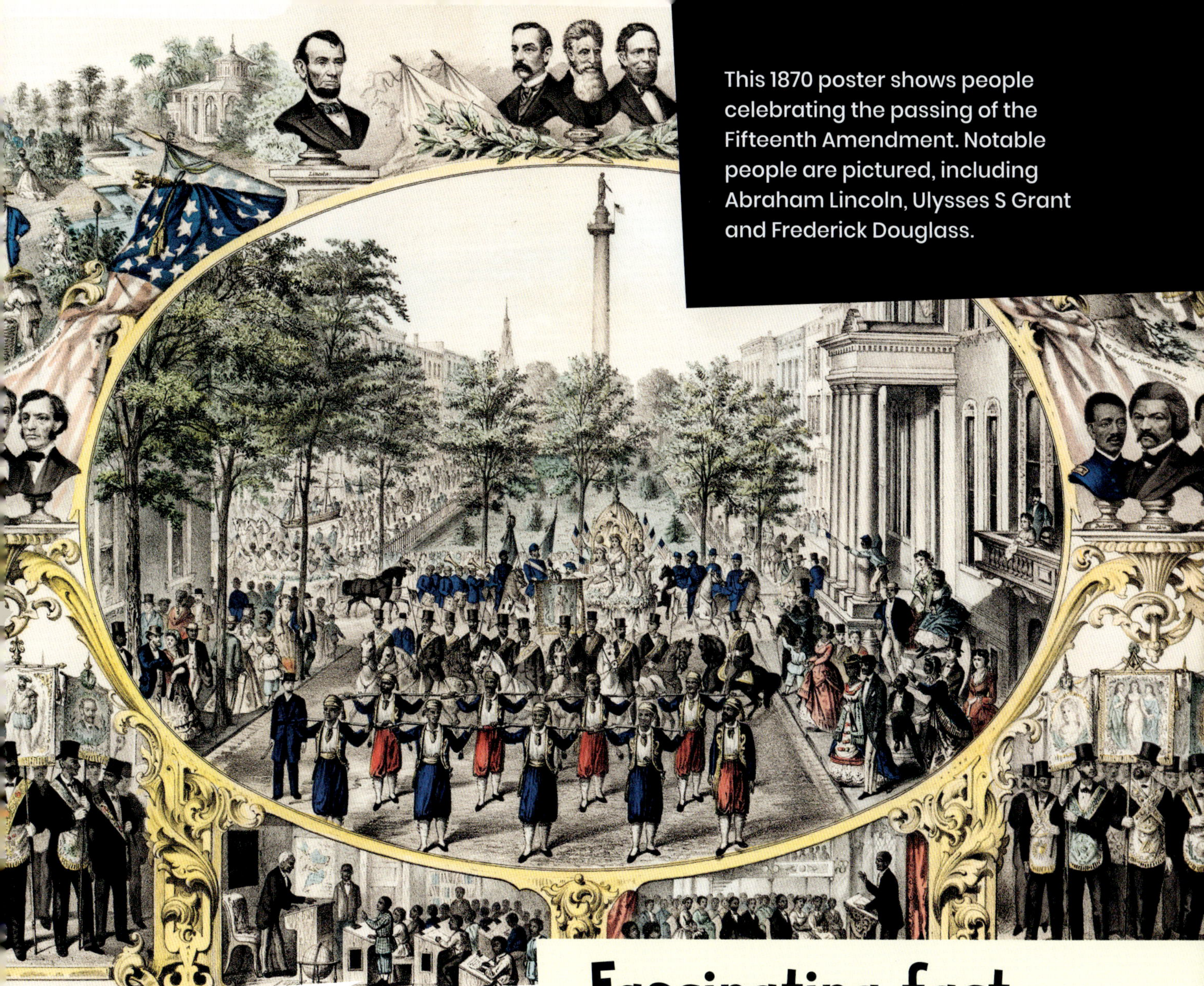

This 1870 poster shows people celebrating the passing of the Fifteenth Amendment. Notable people are pictured, including Abraham Lincoln, Ulysses S Grant and Frederick Douglass.

Fascinating fact

Lucy Stone married Henry Browne Blackwell in 1855. When reading her wedding vows, she agreed to love and honour her husband, but not to obey him. She was also the first woman in the United States to refuse to take her husband's surname.

RIVAL ASSOCIATIONS

Other activists disagreed with Anthony. They did not think universal suffrage was possible yet. The disagreement caused many members to leave the National Woman Suffrage Association (NWSA). They formed the American Woman Suffrage Association (AWSA) in 1869. Lucy Stone was its most prominent leader. The AWSA supported the Fifteenth Amendment, and was committed to working towards a separate amendment for women's suffrage.

Backlash Against Women's Rights

Many people did not support women's right to vote. Journalists wrote articles criticising the idea of women's suffrage, artists created cartoons to make fun of it and religious leaders spoke out against it. Susan B Anthony decided to take matters into her own hands. On 5 November 1872, she voted. She claimed the Fourteenth Amendment granted her the privileges of citizenship, including the right to vote. Two weeks after voting, she was arrested.

Fascinating fact

Some people claimed that if women were allowed to vote, they might start growing beards.

ANTI-SUFFRAGE ARGUMENTS

At the time, many people did not see men and women as equal. They thought women should not go to university. They especially did not think women should have a say in how society was run. They believed that women were meant to have children and lead the household. Men were meant to lead society. Anti-suffragists felt it was unnatural for women to vote. Some feared voting would cause women to stop caring for their families. Others worried it would **corrupt** women.

THE DAILY GRAPHIC

AN ILLUSTRATED EVENING NEWSPAPER.

VOL. I—NO. 81. NEW YORK, THURSDAY, JUNE 5, 1873. FIVE CENTS

This cartoon was published in *The Daily Graphic* on 5 June 1873. It is mocking Anthony. The caption says, "The woman who dared".

This 1913 photo shows a group of anti-suffrage leaders. They did not believe women should have the right to vote. They thought women should focus on their families. The men in their lives could represent them at the **ballot** box.

ANTI-SUFFRAGE PUBLICATIONS AND ASSOCIATIONS

By the 1880s, anti-suffrage publications and groups were formed. They hoped to prevent women from getting the right to vote. The first issue of *The Anti-Suffragist* was published in July 1908. Three years later, Josephine Dodge founded the National Association Opposed to Woman Suffrage in New York. It soon started its own publication called *Woman's Protest.*

This poster is from 1915. It is one of many cartoons from the time that mocked women's desire to vote.

Casting Her Vote

Susan B Anthony
Anti-slavery and women's rights campaigner

Henry Selden
Susan B Anthony's lawyer

Judge Ward Hunt
Associate justice of the US Supreme Court

Election registrars
Officials in charge of registering people to vote

US marshal
Officer responsible for carrying out arrest warrants for federal courts

Rochester, New York. By 1872, Susan B Anthony was an experienced campaigner for votes for women.

Rochester News
Register to VOTE

Excitement was building for the presidential election.

1 November was a voter registration day.

Register To VOTE

Now is the chance to make our voices heard.

Women across Rochester followed Anthony's lead and went to register to vote.
As the law was unclear, some women persuaded officials to let them register. Others were turned away.
The election took place on 5 November.
I wish to cast my vote.
Anthony wrote to Elizabeth Cady Stanton about her success.
I have done it! I voted this morning at 7 o'clock.
We will go to the courts for the women who were not allowed to vote.

Two weeks after the election.
Is this the home of Miss Susan B Anthony?
I am sorry, Miss Anthony, but it is my unpleasant duty to serve a warrant for your arrest.
Very well, I will go with you, but you've got to arrest me properly - handcuffs and all!
Anthony appeared in court with other women who had voted in the election.
The charge is knowingly voting without a right to vote.
It says that the courtroom looked more like a social gathering.
It also says that we are neglecting our household duties!
They still do not think we're serious.

I will never pay a dollar of your unjust penalty.

Although Anthony lost in court, it was an important step on the long road to votes for women.

Susan B Anthony's trial helped make her famous across the nation.

United Again

Susan B Anthony and other activists continued to work towards women's suffrage. In 1878, Anthony wrote an amendment for Congress to consider. It was not passed and was reintroduced every year for 42 years. Each time it was ignored or voted against.

This is the headquarters of the National American Woman Suffrage Association in New York City around 1913.

REUNITED...

In 1890, after more than 20 years as separate organisations, the two major women's suffrage groups joined forces. They formed the National American Woman Suffrage Association. Two years later, Anthony became its president. Despite her earlier opposition to the Fifteenth Amendment, many activists supported Anthony.

...BUT STILL DIVIDED

Suffragists had reunited, but Black American women were often left out. In the South, they were discouraged from attending meetings. They were **segregated** when marching in parades. In 1892, Helen Appo Cook formed a group to give Black women a voice. It was called the National League of Colored Women. This was followed by the National Association of Colored Women in 1896. These and other organisations worked towards suffrage and **civil rights**.

Ida B Wells was a renowned journalist and activist. She founded the Alpha Suffrage Club of Chicago in 1913.

SOCIAL CHANGE

From 1880 to 1910, the number of working women in the United States tripled from 2.6 million to 7.8 million. Women's job prospects and pay were limited compared to men's. Nonetheless, women secured important rights. Married women were granted the right to control the money they made. They could own property. If they divorced, women could keep **custody** of their children.

A NEW STRATEGY

While the federal government did not give women the right to vote, it was still possible for individual states to pass women's suffrage laws. Wyoming was the first, in 1869. From the 1890s to the 1910s, several others followed. As a result, suffragists switched their focus to individual states. They hoped that if enough states supported their right to vote, the government would be forced to do the same.

Fascinating fact

When the Statue of Liberty was unveiled in 1886, a boat carrying nearly 200 women sailed by. They held a sign that read, "American women have no liberty".

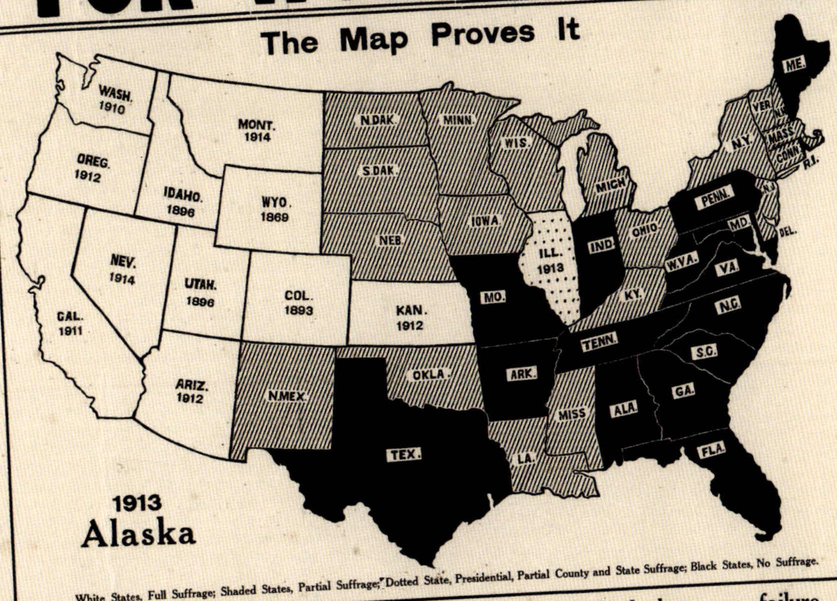

This campaign poster shows the states that had granted women the right to vote, and in what year.

Last Steps to the Vote

Susan B Anthony asked Ida Husted Harper to write an official biography about her life and work. The first part was published in 1898. Two years later, Anthony retired as president of the National American Woman Suffrage Association. She was 80 years old. At the time, she said the movement needed "stronger hands, younger heads, and fresher hearts" (Lutz, 1959).

Carrie Chapman Catt took over as president after Anthony retired. Born in 1859, she was a prominent leader in the movement.

Anthony met President Roosevelt and urged him to submit an amendment for women's suffrage to Congress. It would be another 14 years before this would come to pass.

CONTINUED WORK

Although Anthony retired, she continued working towards suffrage. In 1905, she met President Theodore Roosevelt to discuss women's suffrage. At her 86th birthday celebration in February 1906, she gave a speech that has become famous, in which she declared, "Failure is impossible!" (Sherr, 1995). Anthony died less than one month later from heart failure and pneumonia. Other activists continued to work towards the right that she had dedicated her life to achieving.

A MORE RADICAL APPROACH

After Anthony's death, a new wave of suffragists joined the fight for women's rights. Alice Paul was one of them. She was unhappy with the National American Woman Suffrage Association's focus on states. So, she formed the National Woman's Party. It worked to push Congress to sign women's voting rights into law. Paul organised parades and **pickets**. This included the first ever **protest** at the White House. The protests were peaceful, but Paul was arrested and treated very badly in jail. As news of her treatment spread, more people started to support women's suffrage.

Alice Paul

On 3 March 1913, approximately 8,000 women marched with banners and floats to the White House. Half a million people watched them. Some spectators supported them, but some harassed the marchers.

This photo shows women picketing following Alice Paul's arrest. In jail, Paul and other suffragists were beaten. She was force-fed through a tube after refusing to eat.

The Susan B Anthony Amendment

World War I took place from 1914 to 1918. While American men fought in Europe, many women worked as nurses to help wounded soldiers. At home in the United States, women performed jobs that had traditionally been done by men. This proved that women could contribute to society, and not just in their households. It showed that women were worthy of being considered equal to men.

Think about it

The Nineteenth Amendment, which called for women's suffrage, was also known as the "Susan B Anthony Amendment". Why do you think the amendment was given this name, 14 years after Anthony's death?

President Woodrow Wilson did not originally support women's rights or equal rights for Black American people. He changed his mind about women's suffrage for political reasons. He thought if he opposed it, his party would lose votes in the next election.

Sixty-sixth Congress of the United States of America;

At the First Session,

Begun and held at the City of Washington on Monday, the nineteenth day of May, one thousand nine hundred and nineteen.

JOINT RESOLUTION

Proposing an amendment to the Constitution extending the right of suffrage to women.

Resolved by the Senate and House of Representatives of the United States of America in Congress assembled (two-thirds of each House concurring therein), That the following article is proposed as an amendment to the Constitution, which shall be valid to all intents and purposes as part of the Constitution when ratified by the legislatures of three-fourths of the several States.

"ARTICLE ——.

"The right of citizens of the United States to vote shall not be denied or abridged by the United States or by any State on account of sex.

"Congress shall have power to enforce this article by appropriate legislation."

F. H. Gillett

Speaker of the House of Representatives.

The Nineteenth Amendment was ratified on 18 August 1920. It reads, "The right of citizens of the United States to vote shall not be denied or abridged by the United States or by any State on account of sex".

THE NINETEENTH AMENDMENT

In 1918, Congress voted on the Nineteenth Amendment. To pass, three-quarters of states needed to approve it. The states that had already given women voting rights supported the amendment, but it did not get enough votes until 1920. Tennessee had the deciding vote. Harry Burn, a 24-year-old legislator, decided to cast his vote in favour of the amendment to **appease** his mother.

FIRST-TIME VOTERS AND VOTER SUPPRESSION

On 2 November 1920, more than eight million women voted for the first time. However, many people were still denied this right. The states of Mississippi and Georgia claimed women had missed their chance to register and refused to allow women to vote in the 1920 election. In other parts of the nation, some Black American, Asian American, Hispanic American and **Indigenous** women were also prevented from voting.

This photo shows women in Washington, DC, voting for the first time.

A Long Road to Equality

The vote was just one victory on the road to full rights for women. They were still far from being treated equally. Susan B Anthony, Elizabeth Cady Stanton and others had worked hard to achieve women's suffrage. People stepped up to continue their important work.

The League of Women Voters was founded by suffragists from the National American Woman Suffrage Association.

THE LEAGUE OF WOMEN VOTERS

The League of Women Voters was formed in 1920 in Chicago. It was founded shortly before the Nineteenth Amendment was ratified. Its purpose was to help women vote. It continues working towards voting rights and equal rights today.

Think about it

Can you think of ways that men and women are still treated differently today?

The **gender pay gap** describes the fact that, in general, men are paid more than women, even when they do the same job. In the United States, for every $1 that a white man makes, a white woman makes 83 cents, a Black woman makes 70 cents and a Hispanic woman makes 65 cents.

The aim of the Equal Rights Amendment is that everyone will be treated the same, regardless of their gender.

WORKERS' RIGHTS AND EQUAL PAY

Many groups continue to campaign for workers' rights and equal pay for women. For example, **maternity leave** and **affordable** childcare are important issues. Debates continue over the gender pay gap in the worlds of business, professional sports and more. People continue to disagree on important issues such as child marriage, which is legal in several US states, and women's **reproductive rights**.

EQUAL RIGHTS AMENDMENT

The Equal Rights Amendment was introduced more than 100 years ago. It was written by Alice Paul and an activist named Crystal Eastman. They wanted to protect the rights of women in the US Constitution. Today, some people hope the Equal Rights Amendment will become the Twenty-Eighth Amendment. However, others are concerned that it could cause women to be drafted into the military. They worry that it could negatively impact divorced women and their children.

Lessons from History

Many people have worked toward different causes throughout history, but Susan B Anthony remains an important figure in the history of women's suffrage. So what can we learn from how Anthony lived and the choices she made?

This image shows suffragists demonstrating in New York during World War I.

THE POWER OF PROTEST

The women's suffrage movement involved many people. They worked peacefully together for a long period of time. Change did not occur as quickly as the suffragists would have liked, but they did not give up. Their determination and hard work laid the groundwork for success. They knew others would continue their work, and someday, it would make a difference.

This photo from 1915 shows suffragists marching to gain support for women's rights.

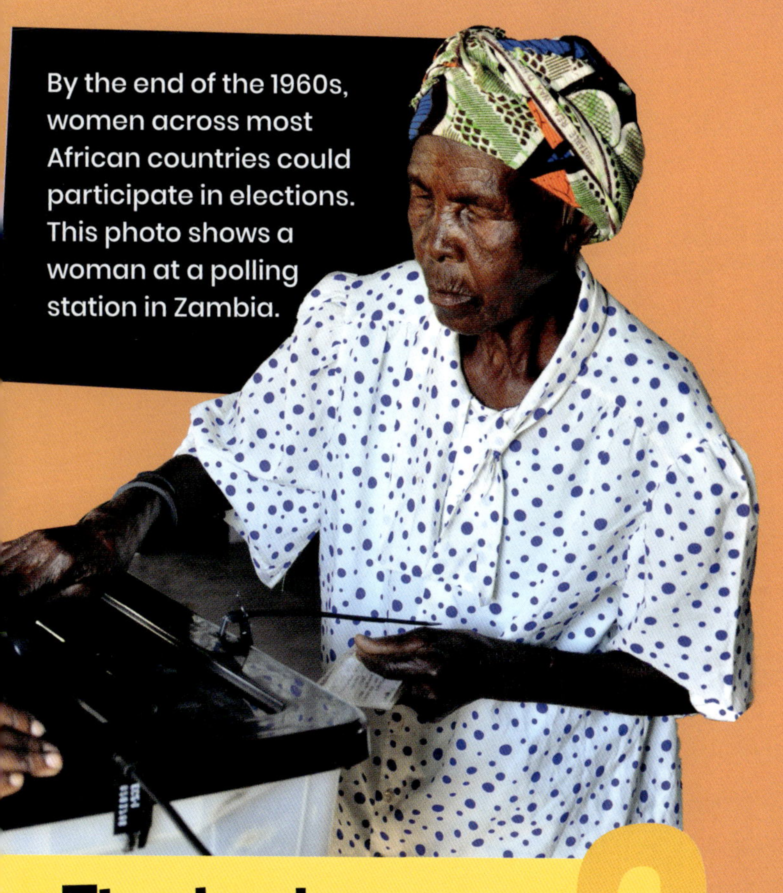

By the end of the 1960s, women across most African countries could participate in elections. This photo shows a woman at a polling station in Zambia.

THE POTENTIAL FOR SOCIETY TO CHANGE

The idea that women could vote was once considered outrageous. Today, this is a fact of life. This shows that society has the potential to change. The speed of progress has varied in different parts of the world. Some conservative countries in Southwest Asia did not give women the right to vote until the 21st century.

THE IMPORTANCE OF VOTING RIGHTS

Anthony and others worked to gain multiple rights for women, but voting rights became their focus. They recognised that women's right to vote was the key. It would open the door to shaping society. When people vote today, they help make decisions about human rights, education, the economy, the environment and more.

Think about it

What movements can you think of that are important in today's society?

Activists work today to protect voting rights for all American people, and encourage citizens to make use of their right to vote.

Uncovering the Truth

A lot is known about the people and events of the women's rights movement. This is because there are so many primary and secondary sources available. A primary source is a document or object created at the time of a historical event. A secondary source is a document or object created after the event, or by someone who was not directly involved in it. They can explain or interpret primary sources. They help in understanding an event.

Primary sources include

- official documents
- letters
- diaries
- paintings or drawings
- photographs
- sound recordings
- videos

Secondary sources include

- news articles
- books
- media documentaries
- encyclopaedias

Photo of original source

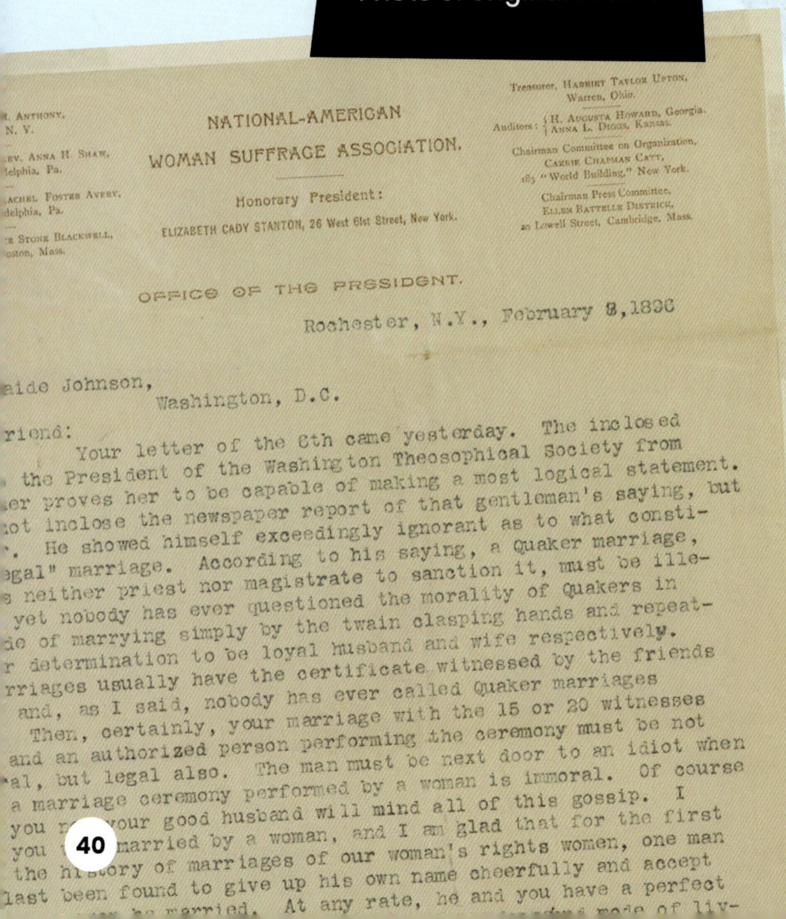

DIFFERENT POINTS OF VIEW

Primary and secondary sources may tell different stories depending on the views of the people who created them. A suffragist would have a different perspective from an anti-suffragist. It is important to question sources – doing this helps us to understand them and understand different perspectives better.

LETTER

This document is a primary source. It is a letter **dictated** by Susan B Anthony in 1896. In this letter, Anthony responds to her friend Adelaide Johnson, congratulating her on her recent marriage. Johnson and her husband had been married by a woman, and Johnson's husband decided to take her last name.

Extract from original source text

My dear Friend:
Your letter of the 6th came yesterday [...]

You did not inclose the newspaper report of that gentleman's saying, but no matter. He showed himself exceedingly ignorant as to what constitutes "legal" marriage.

According to his saying, a Quaker marriage, which has neither priest nor magistrate to sanction it, must be illegal, and yet nobody has ever questioned the morality of Quakers in their mode of marrying simply by the twain clasping hands and repeating their determination to be loyal husband and wife respectively. These marriages usually have the certificate witnessed by the friends present, and, as I said, nobody has ever called Quaker marriages immoral. Then, certainly, your marriage with the 15 or 20 witnesses present and an authorized person performing the ceremony must be not only moral, but legal also [...]

I am glad you were married by a woman, and I am glad that for the first time in the history of marriages of our woman's rights women, one man has at last been found to give up his own name cheerfully and accept that of the woman he married [...]

Anthony mentions a man who criticised Johnson's marriage for not being legal.

She compares Johnson's marriage to a typical Quaker marriage.

She gives her opinion on the two things that were unusual about Johnson's marriage.

Look at the letter, then read the transcribed version of the text and answer the questions below.

Quick questions

- What word does Anthony use to describe the man who criticised Johnson's marriage?
- How does Anthony feel about Johnson's husband taking her name, instead of the other way around?

Discussion questions

- Why do you think Anthony uses the example of a Quaker marriage when discussing whether Johnson's marriage is legal or not? What is her argument?
- This letter was written in 1896. Based on what you have learned, what was the state of women's rights in American society at this time?

- Ignorant.
- She is glad and thinks it is the first time it has happened among the women's rights activists she knows.

Vocabulary Builder A Continued Campaign

What might a publication in favour of women's suffrage look like? Read this fictional pamphlet to see what a persuasive suffragist might have written. Pay attention to key words that describe the movement and try to convince others to support it.

A Continued Campaign

MARCH 1917

For years, campaigners have petitioned Congress to pass an amendment in support of women's suffrage. It is past time for the federal government to give us the right to cast our ballots. Countless activists have written letters, signed petitions, marched, picketed, protested and more. We have given speeches at conferences, debated the issue and **boycotted** the businesses of those who oppose it. Many of us have worked to abolish slavery and allow all men the right to vote. Yet women are still discriminated against and excluded from politics. We should have the right to help choose our representatives, too. Many states have ratified a woman's right to vote into their constitutions, yet others continue to prohibit it. We urge you to advocate for women's suffrage so that we may enjoy the right to vote alongside all other citizens in this country we call home.

Imagine you are writing a pamphlet in the 1910s to convince people to support suffrage, for women or for another group who are not yet allowed to vote. Then use the pamphlet on page 42 and the prompts and word bank below to write your own pamphlet.

- **How do you feel about the right to vote?**
- **What action can be taken?**
- **What language can you use to persuade people to support the cause?**

Protest	activists, boycott, conference, demonstration, letters, march, petition, picket, speech, vote
Actions	abolish, advocate, campaign, debate, discriminate, exclude, include, oppose, prohibit, support
Political terms	amendment, ballot, Congress, constitution, federal government, politics, ratify, representative, states

Glossary

Abolished To have ended or stopped.

Abolition A movement working to end or stop something, for example, slavery.

Abolitionist Someone who worked to end slavery.

Activist Someone who works for or against an issue or cause.

Advocate To work in support of an issue or cause.

Affordable To be relatively inexpensive.

Amendment A change in a law. In the United States, it is also an official change to the US Constitution.

Anti-suffragist Someone against women's suffrage.

Appease To give in to someone's demands.

Association An organisation of people working together with a shared purpose.

Ballot A paper on which people record their vote.

Boycotted The act of not buying or not using something from a company or country to show you disagree with its beliefs, policies or methods. For example, if people do not like how a company treats its workers, they might stop buying its products to force it to change.

Campaigning Doing a series of activities to support or oppose an issue or cause.

Citizen Someone who lives in a country and is entitled to certain rights and responsibilities as a result.

Civil rights The rights and freedoms granted to the citizens of a country.

Congress A body of government in the United States charged with discussing ideas and making decisions. It is made up of the Senate and the House of Representatives.

Constitution The written laws that govern a country. The United States has separate constitutions for each state, in addition to the United States Constitution that applies to the entire country.

Convention A gathering of people for a specific purpose. Also called a conference.

Corrupt To cause bad or immoral behaviour.

Custody The duty to care for someone or something, for example, a child.

Declaration of Independence The document that marked the independence of the American colonies from Great Britain and the founding of the United States.

Delegation A group of people who represent a larger group.

Dictated Speech that is written down.

Discrimination Unfair treatment due to prejudice.

Earnest To be serious and determined.

Election A process in which the public chooses their leaders and helps make decisions.

Enslaved To be forced to work for someone else without the freedom to stop or leave.

Equality To have the same rights as others and be seen as equals.

Forged To be made, created or crafted.

Gender pay gap The difference in average pay between men and women.

House of Representatives One of the two chambers of Congress that makes and passes federal laws. It has 435 representatives who can cast votes.

Indigenous Indigenous peoples are groups of people who are the original inhabitants of a region or area. There may be many different groups of Indigenous peoples within a region, each with their own languages and cultures.

Industrialisation The process in the 18th and 19th centuries that led to a rise in the invention of machines and building of factories, and a move towards large-scale manufacturing.

Injustice Unfairness, inequality or discrimination.

Maternity leave A period of time off work granted to new mothers after the birth of a child.

Menial To be unskilled or unimportant.

Movement A campaign of activities working to achieve a common goal.

Opposed To be against or in disagreement with something, such as an idea or action.

Petition A written request or demand for change, often including signatures of supporters.

Picket To protest by standing in place.

Pivotal An important turning point.

Politics Practices related to government.

Progressive To be interested in new or modern ideas and supportive of change.

Prohibit To prevent, stop or forbid.

Protest To show disagreement in actions or words.

Ratified To be approved or signed into law.

Representative An elected official who acts on behalf of people by attending official meetings and voting.

Reproductive rights Rights related to pregnancy and childbirth.

Segregated To be kept separate due to gender, race, religion or other factors.

Slavery A system in which people are owned by their enslavers and forced to work without pay.

Source A written document, artefact or building that provides information relating to the past. Sources are also known as evidence.

Suffrage The ability to vote.

Suffragist Someone who supported women's right to vote.

Temperance A movement that supported limiting or banning alcohol.

Vote To formally give an opinion on something.

Index

Acknowledgments

The publisher would like to thank the following for their kind permission to reproduce their photographs:

(Key: a-above; b-below/bottom; c-center; f-far; l-left; r-right; t-top)

4-5 Alamy Stock Photo: Shawshots (t). **4 Alamy Stock Photo:** World History Archive (bl). **Mary Evans Picture Library:** Vernon Lewis Gallery / Stocktrek Images (c). **6 Alamy Stock Photo:** Pictorial Press Ltd (c); Science History Images (b). **7 Alamy Stock Photo:** Underwood Archives, Inc (br). **8 Alamy Stock Photo:** IanDagnall Computing (br); Universal Images Group North America LLC (cl). **9 Alamy Stock Photo:** Everett Collection Inc (bl); IanDagnall Computing (br). **10-11 Getty Images:** Bettmann (t); Frank Ramspott (c). **10 Alamy Stock Photo:** Zeytun Travel Images (bl). **11 Alamy Stock Photo:** Randy Duchaine (br). **12 Alamy Stock Photo:** North Wind Picture Archives (b). **13 Alamy Stock Photo:** GL Archive (br); Glasshouse Images (tl). **14 Bridgeman Images:** Schlesinger Library, Radcliffe Institute, Harvard (b). **15 Alamy Stock Photo:** North Wind Picture Archives (b). **Bridgeman Images:** North Wind Pictures (t). **16 Alamy Stock Photo:** Granger Historical Picture Archive (bl). **17 Alamy Stock Photo:** Granger Historical Picture Archive (b); Science History Images (t). **18 Alamy Stock Photo:** World History Archive (b). **19 Alamy Stock Photo:** incamerastock (t); Pictorial Press Ltd (b). **20 Alamy Stock Photo:** North Wind Picture Archives (c). Library of Congress, Washington, D.C.: (b). **21 Alamy Stock Photo:** Rye Hobie (b). Getty Images: MPI (t). **22 Alamy Stock Photo:** Randy Duchaine (b); Science History Images (t). **23 Alamy Stock Photo:** incamerastock (t). 24 Library of Congress, Washington, D.C.. **25 Alamy Stock Photo:** FLHC26 (t). Bridgeman Images: Granger (b). **30 Alamy Stock Photo:** Alpha Historica (b); Imago History Collection (t). **31 Alamy Stock Photo:** CBW (b). **32 Alamy Stock Photo:** Pictorial Press Ltd (b); Science History Images (t). **33 Alamy Stock Photo:** Everett Collection Historical (t); Realy Easy Star (bl). **Mary Evans Picture Library:** Glasshouse Images (br). **34 Alamy Stock Photo:** Archive Pics. **35 Alamy Stock Photo:** Pictorial Press Ltd (t); World History Archive (b). **36 Alamy Stock Photo:** John Candler Lazenby (b). **37 Alamy Stock Photo:** Sipa US (b). **Getty Images:** Marc Atkins (t). **38 Alamy Stock Photo:** Granger Historical Picture Archive (t); Shawshots (b). **39 Alamy Stock Photo:** Associated Press (b). Dreamstime.com: Smandy (t). **40 Library of Congress, Washington, D.C.:** Susan B. Anthony Papers (b). **43 Alamy Stock Photo:** RKive (t).

Cover images: *Front:* **Alamy Stock Photo:** American Photo Archive b, The Granger Collection c; **Dreamstime.com:** Yuri Arcurs br; Getty Images / iStock: E4C t/ (background); *Back:* **Alamy Stock Photo:** Shawshots b, World History Archive t, Zeytun Travel Images c.

Quote attributions:

Griffith, Elizabeth. 1984. *In Her Own Right:* The Life of Elizabeth Cady Stanton. Oxford University Press.
Lutz, Alma. 1959. *Susan B. Anthony: Rebel, Crusader, Humanitarian.* Beacon Press.
Sherr, Lynn. 1995. *Failure is Impossible: Susan B. Anthony in Her Own Words*. Times Books.

All the books in the DK Super History series have been reviewed by authenticity readers to ensure the represented cultures and experiences are accurate.

This book uses language as appropriate to modern contexts. Historical terms that are no longer acceptable may be present in original source materials and images. These sources are included to present authentic insights into history.